Senior Centre

by
Linda Kita-Bradley

Grass Roots Press

Text Copyright © 2014 Grass Roots Press

All rights reserved. No part of this book may be reproduced or transmitted in any form or by any means, including photocopy, recording, or any information storage and retrieval system, without the prior written permission of the publisher.

Senior Centre is published by
Grass Roots Press, a division of Literacy Services of Canada Ltd.

www.grassrootsbooks.net

ACKNOWLEDGMENTS

We acknowledge the financial support of the Government of Canada through the Canada Book Fund (CBF) for our publishing activities.

Produced with the assistance of the Government of Alberta, Alberta Multimedia Development Fund.

Alberta Government

Editor: Dr. Pat Campbell
Photography: Grass Roots Press
Book design: Lara Minja, Lime Design Inc.

Library and Archives Canada Cataloguing in Publication

Kita-Bradley, Linda, 1958–, author
    Senior centre / Linda Kita-Bradley.

ISBN 978-1-77153-037-8 (pbk.)

    1. Readers for new literates. 2. Readers—Senior centers. I. Title.

PE1126.N43K58717 2014   428.6'2   C2014-903962-X

This is Sara.

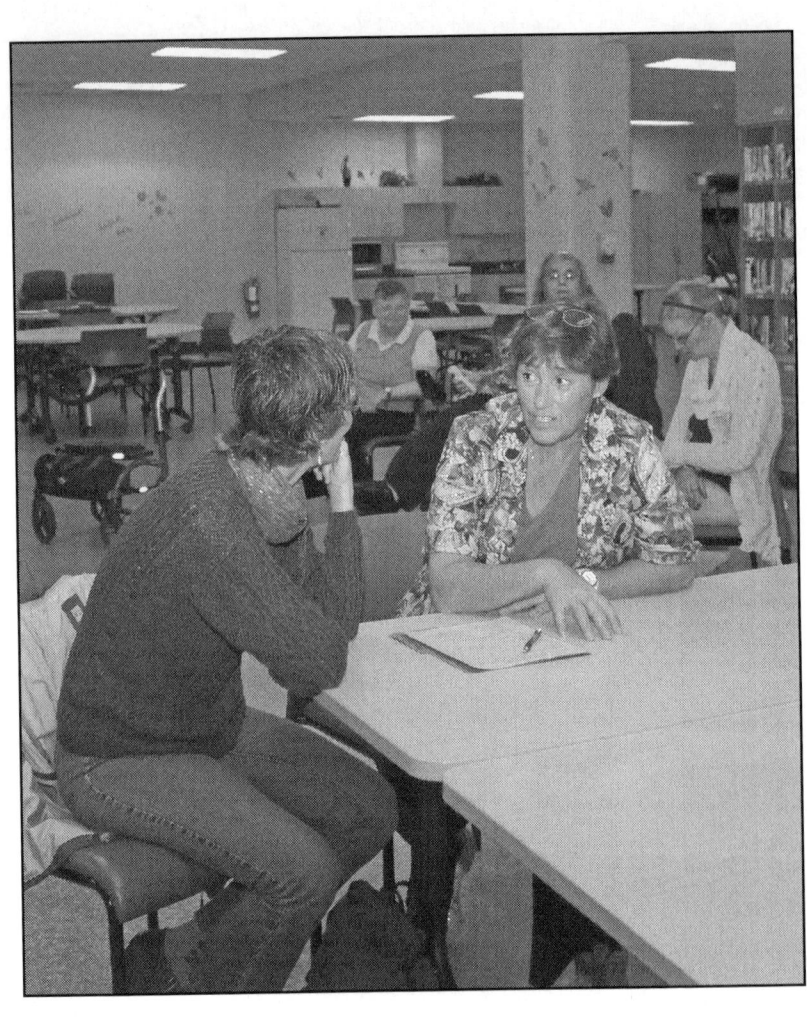

Sara volunteers for a senior centre.

The centre reaches out to seniors at home.

This is Jay.
Jay lives alone.

Sara visits Jay on Mondays.

They play cards.

They have tea.

They talk.

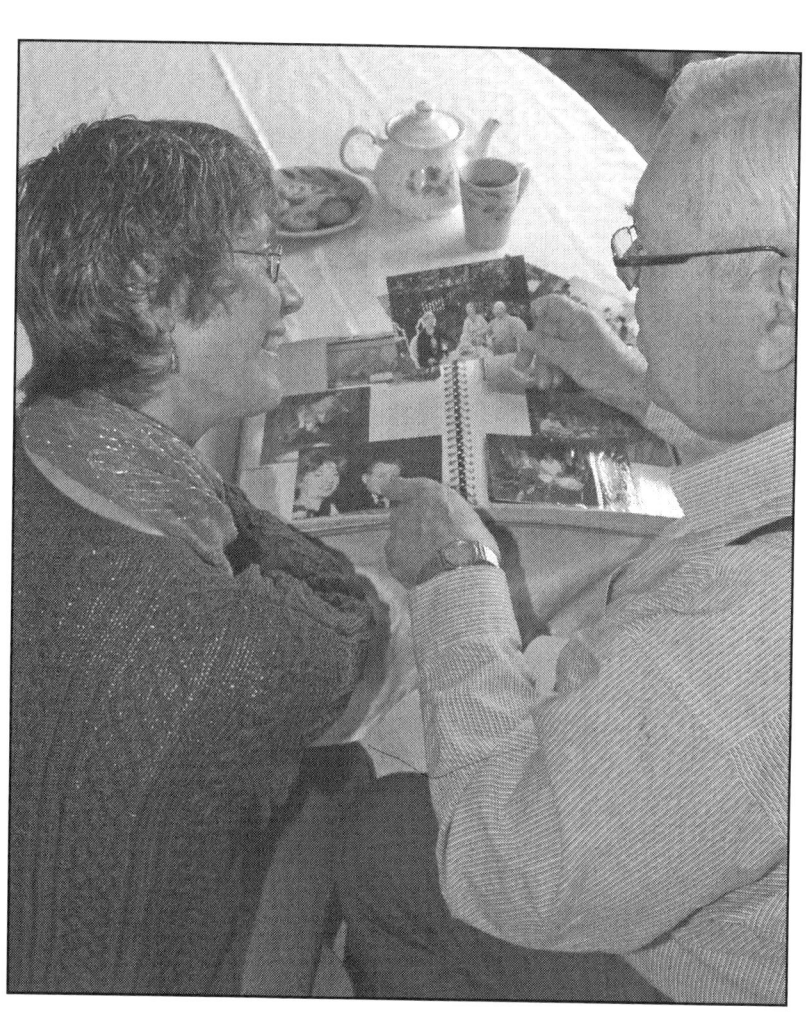

Jay talks about his family.
He talks about his life.

"I was a painter," says Jay.
"A long time ago."

"What! Can you teach me?"

Jay finds his paint set.

He wipes off the dust.

Jay and Sara start to paint.

Sara makes a mess.

Jay helps Sara try again.

Sara stops at the senior centre.

"I'm learning to paint!"

They talk about Sara's visit.

The staff person takes notes.

She adds the notes to Sara's file.

At home, Jay is still painting.

Made in the USA
Columbia, SC
07 February 2022